LONDON BUS DIARY OF 1991-1992

by

R. J. Waterhouse

Series editor
Alan Townsin

Transport Publishing Co Ltd : Glossop : Derbyshire : England

ISBN 086317 176 1

Since it was founded in 1973 the Transport Publishing Company has published a large number of books on the British Bus Industry. Although many of the earlier titles are now unfortunately out of print, a wide range of books covering operators and manufacturers is still available. Full details of all titles in print available from the Publishers.

Designed, typeset and produced for the Publishers by Mopok Graphics, 128 Pikes Lane, Glossop, Derbyshire
Printed and bound in Great Britain

Contents

South London's RML 895, one of the first batch of 30ft. Routemasters dating from 1961, became the first production vehicle to go through the new refurbishment programme. It was 'launched' on 26th February 1992 after arrival from TB Precision Engineering but on 13th March, the day Streatham garage closed, worked a few turns on routes 118 and 349 from that garage, though those routes and indeed the whole of Streatham's final workings were OPO. In this view, it is seen loading outside the garage for the first of its journeys on 118. Traditionalists will be reassured that external changes are minimal.

The first new class to enter service in 1991 consisted of eight Reebur-bodied Iveco midibuses for routes H24 and H25 from Feltham to Hatton Cross and Hanworth. These are unusual on several counts, not least the London Borough of Hounslow's white and green colours (they own these buses) but also that they can take one wheelchair passenger (one of Hounslow's requirements for the routes) facilitated by the rear-mounted wheelchair lift. These shots are of FR 4 in Bedfont Lane and the rear of FR 5 at Hanworth Park, showing the wheelchair entry.

January

It was announced that London Buses was expected to cut £3million from its £400million budget because of what was described as a 'cash crisis', which was blamed on the collapse of the London property market because of the economic recession, and it was thought that cuts would have to be made on early-morning and late-morning services.

London Buses announced a £900,000 programme of fitting a new safety device made by Wilfred Overton of Wednesbury to the centre exit doors of 2,882

Another operator new to Harrow was BTS Coaches, whose poppy-red Leyland Olympians bodied by Northern Counties took over the 114. This one, caught at Ruislip Manor, works the Sunday extension to Ruislip Lido, always popular on Summer Sundays, not so in bleak January! London Buses subsidiary Metroline won less than half the routes put out to tender, but enough midibus routes to justify an allocation of LBL's Dennis Dart delivery to the North Wembley outstation of its Harrow Weald garage. The representative here is DT 119, with Carlyle body caught near Pinner on the first day.

The other major scheme this month started the same day, in Bexleyheath. Kentishbus gained three routes from London Central, the LBL subsidiary that back in November took over Bexleyheath garage from Selkent as it had won most of the routes put out to tender. On the 96 and 269, ECW-bodied Olympians formerly from Northumbria and originally new to United Automobile Services were moved in. This one is 311, seen at Plumstead.

buses. By April 1993 new legislation will require all buses built since April 1980. If an object gets caught in the exit doors on closing, the doors reopen automatically.

LBL subsidiary London Forest announced a rolling programme to fit reconditioned low-pullutant emission 'green' engines to its Leyland Titan fleet.

On the road, new route contracts began in the Harrow and Bexley areas.

New Optare Metroriders were ordered for Kentishbus's other new route, the B11, however only one had arrived by the start date and two demonstrators were to be seen for the first few weeks. One of the demonstrators and 886 are seen in Bexleyheath here on 26th January.

Transcity Coaches were a new operator to the LRT fray, and with their Talbot Pullman triaxles make a good job of the B15, their only route. The livery is green with yellow relief.

As loss-making Boroline Maidstone had gained route 272 in November, with that contract requiring new or new-ish vehicles, it needed new buses. This is one of six new Olympians with Northern Counties bodywork which entered service in January.

Unconnected with the Bexley scheme were Selkent's new midibus routes, 380 and 386 in the Woolwich, Plumstead, Abbey Wood, Blackheath, Lewisham and Eltham areas and Sunday conversions to midibus operation of established big bus routes. Fourteen Optare Metroriders commenced operation from Plumstead garage, and MRL 154 works a Sunday duty here in Woolwich. The Optare Metrorider became more popular as the year progressed.

From January 19th night route N94 (Trafalgar Square to Edgware via Kilburn) was renumbered N16 to avoid confusion with day route 94 which ran over some common ground within Central London. Metroline Metrobus M 696 was caught at the Central London end on 3rd March.

The LRT Barnet scheme commenced on February 2nd and, as ever these days, midibus types seemed to feature in the main events. Brand new Dennis Darts with Wright (Ballymena) bodywork were allocated to Leaside Buses' Wood Green garage for the 84A which was retained by that company on tender, and DW 51 is just about to leave a stop in Barnet High Street on the first day.

February

Valentine's day, 14th February, was the day that—at last—smoking became banned on all LRT bus services, following precedents set by other operators. Public Transport Minister Roger Freeman welcomed the ban as 'an important step towards making buses a safer and more attractive form of transport.' Research carried out before it was implemented showed that less than one in five bus passengers actually smoked on buses.

Increased on-bus security measures were implemented on all London Buses vehicles because of the Gulf war. Passengers were allowed to take aboard only luggage which they could hold on to.

The annual Minet TransRisk/ London Buses garage safety contest was won by CentreWest's Uxbridge garage, with Norbiton and Edgware garages coming second and third. Later in the month David Brown, Uxbridge's GGM (Garage General Manager) and part of the winning team, took up a similar post at Hanwell garage.

A new consultation document from London Transport, aimed at the public, asked for comments on key policy issues such as fares, service levels and other priorities for the next few years. The document was issued to local authorities and transport users' groups as well as British Rail and the answers were to be taken into account in LT's new *Statement of Strategy*.

The major change on the roads in February was the initiation of LRT's Barnet area scheme. Most routes involved were London Buses 'block grant' routes, and most of those that survived remained so, a status shared by new routes 326 and 385. Existing Cockfosters-Barnet service 384, originally an LRT contract service, became block grant also, however route 84A from Turnpike Lane to Barnet remained a contract service.

Optare Star Riders displaced from Harrow feature in our next two shots. Route 143 was a straightforward Metrobus to midibus conversion, save for the retention of one M on school journeys renumbered 143A, and SR 104 of Edgware is caught at Gravel Hill. For London Northern's midi-routes the unoriginal 'Midilink' name was used. One of its new routes was the 326 (Brent Cross Shopping Centre to New Barnet Station with projections to Potters Bar Garage) which replaced most of route 26, and SR 102 of Potters Bar is caught in Regents Park Road.

London Northern' s other new service was the 385, a Barnet local service serving the Quinta Drive and Dollis Valley areas for the first time. MCW Metrorider MR 47 of Potters Bar is in the High Street.

Route 125, a tendered route operated by Grey-Green, received a daily extension from North Finchley to Finchley Central to provide a service for passengers who used to travel across North Finchley to and from Whetstone on the 26. Grey-Green 109, a Scania N112 with East Lancs bodywork, is caught in Regents Park Road.

The southern part of the 26 was replaced by an extension on Mondays to Saturdays of route 102 from Golders Green to Brent Cross shopping centre, with the frequency upped on this section as well. M 617 of Palmers Green garage is on that, on the first day.

With the introduction of a new contract on Monday to Saturday route H17 from Harrow to Sudbury (Vale Farm Sports Centre) from 16th February, the Harrow revisions were complete. The attractive buildings of Harrow School provides an excellent backdrop for Sovereign Bus & Coach's Mercedes 811D/Reebur H417 FGS en route for Sudbury on a dismal February 23rd. Previous operators were R. & I. Tours.

The 'red route', 17A from Holloway (Nags Head) to East Finchley on LRT contract, was destined to be short-lived but was none the less introduced as part of the Barner scheme. From Holloway garage, Metrobus M 764 is seen approaching Highgate.

The 137A was introduced to improve reliability on the 137 which had been suffering the effects of traffic: however the Sunday operation is the one depicted here, taking over from the 137 completely between Crystal Palace and Oxford Circus, otherwise the northern terminus was Streatham Hill (Sloane Square evenings). Also the bus type, represented by Streatham's Metrobus M 959, is the Sunday one. Monday to Saturday operation was covered by Brixton with DMSs, later Titans.

February 23rd saw a routeing reshuffle with the 283 converted to midibus with DTs but curtailed to run between East Acton and Hammersmith only, the 290 withdrawn on Mondays to Saturdays between Richmond and Hammersmith and new route 190 introduced on Mondays to Saturdays to run between Richmond and West Brompton (Empress State Building) via Hammersmith to replace the withdrawn parts of both routes. The midibus-converted 283 is illustrated with new Carlyle-bodied Dart DT 160 (Stamford Brook) in Bloemfontein Road, while LX 7 of the batch of Leyland Lynxes displaced from the 283 is at Hammersmith on the first day of the 190. Both vehicles come from Stamford Brook garage.

An interesting commercial operation from Metrobus, excellent operator of some tendered routes in South-East London, commenced on 4th March with the 351 between Bromley and Penge via Beckenham, running Mondays to Saturdays only. With route diagram on the side, Mercedes 709D/Reebur F128 TRU turns out of Tweedy Road in Bromley. This bus originally operated with Metrobus on commercial operations in Gravesend, before going to Kentishbus for a while. Five (of the batch of eight) were bought back by Metrobus for this new and successful route.

March

.....saw what was the announcement of the year for many bus-pundits, and probably Harry Blundred as well. The Secretary of State for Transport, Malcolm Rifkind, revealed plans for the deregulation of London bus services. Proposals featured in the Government's new consultation document, 'A Bus Strategy for London' included the privatisation of all London Buses subsidiaries 14 months after deregulation, the preservation of a London-wide concessionary fares scheme by London boroughs, improvements in traffic conditions for all road users with a review of bus lanes and other priority measures, upgrading the fleets of London Buses' companies and research into the effect on traffic of different types of bus operation. But above all that, the most potentially far-reaching proposal was the initiation of a 'London Bus Executive' to oversee all bus operators and services in London as well as maintaining infrastructure such as bus stops. LT chairman Wilfred Newton pledged to do all he could to get the decision reversed. But it must be said, because no-one else appears to have done so up to now, that all this is dependant on a Conservative victory in the election.....

LBL subsidiary London United announced a special free offer for passengers taking advantage of British Airways' free flight offer on 23rd April. Up for grabs were 1,000 free seats. Airbus seats, that is, the draw for which was linked in with that for 1,000 more attractive free flights.

On the roads CentreWest introduced a batch of those fine Dennis Darts with Wrights (Ballymena) bodywork, officially from March 2nd on Gold Arrow routes 28 from Golders Green to Wandsworth and 31 from Camden Town to Chelsea. On the subject of these buses, classified DW,

On the preceding Saturday (2nd) revisions to CentreWest's Gold Arrow services saw the introduction of the DW Wright-bodied Dennis Darts to the schedules for the first time and the replacement of route 52A with new Gold Arrow service 70 (Acton High Street to Kensington, Monday to Saturday) which used some of the MA-class Mercedes with Alexander bodywork displaced. MA 18 at Notting Hill Gate represent the new operations.

there are people who think the windscreen assembly of the buses makes them look a bit like the RF—I can't for one moment imagine quite why. On the minus side, London General stepped up DMS replacement at its Stockwell and Merton garages, drafting in Metrobuses in readiness for the Wandsworth scheme.

In readiness for the LRT Wandsworth schemes London General began gradual removal of DMS type buses in earnest from its Stockwell and Merton garages. Two routes that were converted to midibus operation in the scheme feature here, with Metrobus M 466 on the 156 and Fleetline D 2563 on the 170 at Clapham Junction on March 2nd, both from Stockwell.

From Merton, Metrobus M 171 is seen at Tooting Broadway.

By this time officially DMS buses had long since been removed from night bus work, but a pleasant surprise (or at least, it was to the author) on the morning of March 3rd was this strange working: Sutton's D 2609 on night route N68 at Trafalgar Square.

Luton & District's (or London Country North West's) new LR-class all-Leyland Olympians began to arrive for the 340, and LR 97 is seen in Stanmore.

Most changes in April were scheduled for the 27th. In South East London, the 199 made a comeback to run between Elephant & Castle and Lewisham via Surrey Quays, taking over from sections of routes 1, 108B and P13 (the latter two in the Pepys Estate area). Titan T 1106 is at Bricklayers Arms on the first day.

April

London Buses, through their Selkent subsidiary, regained another route from the private sector via retendering in the shape of the P4 (Lewisham to Brixton) from 27th April. Wright-bodied Darts were used replacing Kentishbus's Leyland Nationals: DW 62 is in Ladywell Road on the first day.

In spite of the '1,000 free seats' offer (see March) the Airbus services had been threatened with substantial cuts, following a drop in the number of passengers carried of 47%, according to Airbus manager John Kately. However things picked up following the cessation of hostilities in the Gulf, and the Airbus routes carried on as before.

London Central announced a reorganisation in its engineering operations, resulting in the loss of 22 jobs spread across the company. On April 17th, London Central Titan T 1039, working route N79, was in collision with a lorry and toppled over onto its nearside. Twenty people, including the driver, were taken to St. Thomas's Hospital. One person suffered serious head injuries. The lorry driver was later charged with driving without due care and attention.

Route changes in the main centred on South-East London, with route revisions and new routes introduced on April 27th.

Revisions to the time-honoured 161 saw it re-routed to Bromley North Station, exemplified by Bromley's Titan T 883, therefore becoming Woolwich to Bromley North, while new route 161A was introduced to run Woolwich to Petts Wood Station over the withdrawn section of the 161. Thus the two routes provided a 10-minute frequency between Woolwich and Chislehurst (the location of Plumstead's Leylana Olympian L 106) where they went their separate ways.

We move away from the South-East to the North-West of the capital for this one. Metroline removed double-deck operation from the 205 (St. Raphael's Estate, near Neasden to Park Royal Asda) in favour of DT-class Dennis Darts like DT 88 from Willesden garage, caught at the Park Royal end passing R & I Tours' garage. Sunday operation, an LRT contract worked by CentreWest, remained the same.

And back to the South-East again. A temporary allocation of MA Alexander-bodied Mercedes was made to Bromley in April to cover temporary loss of DTs which were away having work done to the doorway steps: that became permanent when the DTs were transferred to London United in May, however the MAs were replaced by new MRL-class Optare Metroriders. MA 41 is in Tweedy Road.

Night route revisions from 23rd saw the N14 extended from Kingston via Surbiton (replacing route N87) to Chessington (World of Adventures) and the N87 rerouted via Kingston to Hampton Court Station, in both instances first-time night services. Metrobuses M 1206 (Putney) and 279 (Stockwell) are your buses here.

The Wandsworth scheme introduced on May 25th is illustrated in this section. The 91 was split in two, H91 between Hounslow West (garage journeys to and from Hounslow) and Hammersmith Broadway, with 391 between Turnham Green (overlapping the H91 between there and Hammersmith) and Fulham Broadway with the section of the 91 on to Wandsworth left unreplaced, covered by other services. The new Dennis Dart buses with Reeve Burgess bodywork forming the DR class entered service for the first time. DR 10 from Hounslow garage is seen on the first day at Hounslow West.

May

Details of new independent market research were released by London Buses regarding measures to speed up buses. Three-quarters of the people surveyed supported the introduction of more bus lanes and almost nine out of ten believed there should be stricter controls against motorists to get them out of their cars and onto buses. A surprising statistic was that regarding the possibility of making car drivers pay to come in to Central London – 38% of people surveyed were for it, 44% against it.

The London Explorer, the ticket that gave you unlimited travel on bus and underground services at any time of day or night, seven days a week (within the Travelcard area of course) made a comeback from May 12th, only it was named 'LT Card' and, whilst allowing travel without time restrictions, it was not valid on Network South East or night bus routes. A 'snip' at £5.50 for all six zones? The price of the more popular One-Day Travelcard for all six zones, with Network South East availability, went up 20p to £3.10.

No doubt about the major route change of the month. The Wandsworth area was expanded to encompass Central London and more when LRT's controversial Wandsworth scheme was introduced on May 25th. Routes were chopped (severely in some instances) and changed all over. For midibus routes associated with the scheme the DR-class midibus was introduced for the first time from Hounslow, Merton, Stockwell and Streatham garages – Dennis Darts with Reeve-Burgess 'Pointer' bodywork. Also route C1, the first midibus route in Central London, was originally scheduled for withdrawal from the same date but reprieved for

Loaned DW 82, a Wright-bodied Dart from Stamford Brook is seen also on the first day at the North End Road market—it was destined for Westbourne Park and Gold Arrow services.

three months while sponsorship was sought for the route to enable it to continue. Regular passengers had protested to LT about the route's withdrawal and some said they would be willing to pay increased fares if it meant retaining the route.

Peak-hour workings on the H37, the renumbered Hounslow-Richmond part of the erstwhile 37, were scheduled for LS-type Leyland Nationals because of the rerouteing direct via St. John's Road in Isleworth taking the route under a low bridge. LS 329 works short.

Between Clapham Junction and Richmond the 337 took over. It was scheduled for Ms from Stockwell garage, but one of the Volvo Citybuses with Northern Counties bodywork, VC 28, turns up on 21st October.

The 270 was introduced between Putney Bridge Station and Mitcham (Cricketers) to replace that part of the 220. Metrobus M 318 on Putney Bridge on the first day.

Earlier on we depicted the 156 and 170 with 'deckers. By way of a 'before and after' here are Darts DRs 32 (Merton) and 51 (Stockwell) in Wandsworth on the routes: the 156 was withdrawn north of Clapham Junction and south of Wimbledon whilst the 170 was withdrawn north of Clapham Junction but at least introduced on Sundays.

The 265 received an extension to Tolworth Broadway every half-hour, with a weekday daytime frequency of 15 minutes as far as the Kingston Vale Asda store, and was also introduced on Sundays. The conversion to midibus operation used brand new Alexander-bodied Mercedes from Putney garage. At the east end of the route, MA 132 is caught on Putney Bridge on the first day.

Another long-established route, the 49, was split into three with midibus 249 taking over between Tooting Bec Station and Crystal Palace and big-bus 349 between West Brompton (Empress State Building) and Streatham Garage leaving the 49 to run Shepherds Bush Green—Clapham Junction. The 249 is Monday—Saturday, the 349 daily and extended to Crystal Palace on Sundays. New Dart DR 25 from Streatham is caught at the Tooting Bec end whilst Metrobus M 949 passes the facade of the Northern Line station, dangerous after dark.

The 44 was split into 344 between London Bridge and Clapham Junction via Elephant & Castle and 44 between Vauxhall and Tooting. Your bus here is M 847 Metrobus from Victoria garage at Southwark Bridge Road on the first day. Sunday allocation was from Merton.

Now here are the bits where the Wandsworth scheme gets into central London! Route 74 was withdrawn between Baker Street and Camden Town and rerouted along the Marylebone Road via Euston to Kings Cross (Metrobus M 760 in Lillie Road on the first day) with new route 274 taking over the withdrawn part of the 74, starting from Marble Arch. Chalk Farm's Titan T 504 crosses the Marylebone Road on the first day.

A re-routeing at County Hall took the 77 to Waterloo, and Merton's Metrobus M 171 arrives there on the first day.

Route 30 was involved in the scheme! It replaced the 77A between Kings Cross and Trafalgar Square when extended to the latter point. The doomed Ash Grove garage sends out Titan T 259 on the first day, photographed at Euston.

The kids are alright—they were catered for with this new school route. The 77C was introduced between Clapham Junction and Putney Heath, with journeys from the former point in the morning, from the latter point in the afternoon. Stockwell's Metrobus M 279 is seen here.

There were other changes, in addition to the Wandsworth scheme. Route C10 was introduced on the same day between Elephant & Castle, where Optare City Pacer OV9 is seen on the first day (yes, your author was very busy on 25th May) and Pimlico via Victoria, to replace part of Red Arrow route 510 which was withdrawn and to provide a new link on to Pimlico. A new Red Arrow, 511, was introduced to cover the southern section of the C1 and provide needed extra capacity for the section. Leyland National LS 448 leaves Waterloo.

Route 267, a trolleybus replacement route, had remained unaltered since conversion in 1962, save for conversion to one-person operation. On 25th May, that changed. The R68 (branded 'Harrier' by London United) was introduced between Richmond and Hampton Court Station, where Fulwell's DT 77 is caught, to leave the 267 to run Fulwell Garage—Hammersmith Broadway.

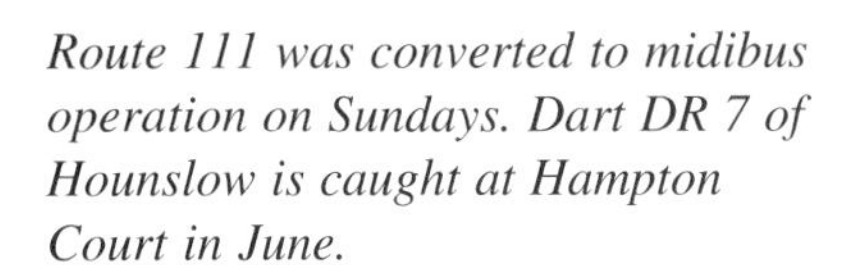

Route 111 was converted to midibus operation on Sundays. Dart DR 7 of Hounslow is caught at Hampton Court in June.

To take the midibus allocation up to the required amount for the 25th May changes at Hounslow, DTs formerly at Bromley were brought in. DT 46 now in its correct Harrier garb is caught on a very hot day in Hounslow High Street.

Monday 10th June saw the introduction of new route U6 from West Drayton Station to Hayes via the Stockley Estate on Mondays to Fridays only via a few new roads in the Stockley Estate area. Alexander-bodied Mercedes-Benz 811D MA 70 attracts attention at West Drayton on the first day.

June

London Buses announced that new louder custom-built assault alarms were to be fitted to all big buses in the fleet; they were to be supplied by J. Maple and Son of Stockport, Cheshire.

Probably louder than the above-mentioned alarms were discussions between London Forest and the Transport and General Workers' Union over the Walthamstow routes, the tenders for which had been awarded to the company—certainly the most pertinent chain of events of the year, and in June it was only just beginning. The T & GWU at least achieved a reduction in the pay-cut 'Forest were attempting to impose, from 21% (big-bus drivers) to 16%, the same figure being allotted to midibus drivers. Ken Fuller, the T & GWU regional officer, called for the management of London Forest to publicly resign.

Four Green Line coach routes, for which London Transport had withdrawn the financial support previously provided, were withdrawn and replaced by new routes. A fifth, the well-known route 726 from Windsor and Slough via Heathrow, Kingston, Sutton and Bromley to Dartford, was formally taken on by LT as a contract service because of its potential usefulness as a bus link across the outskirts of south London. Operation remained with Luton & District, which had taken over from London Country (North West) a year ago, and Kentishbus. The Green Lines withdrawn were the 714 (Kingston to Horsham), 715 (Guildford to Oxford Circus on Mon-Sat, Victoria Suns), 716 (Sunday route, Staines to West Croydon) and 718 (Windsor to Victoria). Another Green Line affected, the 727 (previously Heathrow Central—Crawley) was truncated to run Kingston to Crawley only, with the Sunday service reduced even more to one round journey, albeit extended to Brighton. LT involvement with the scheme, which commenced on June 29th, can be seen in the photograph section.

Ensign Citybus actually lost a tendered route on 22nd June, after a long run of gaining routes on tender. East London took it on with Barking-based Titans. Here's T 228 in The Drive, near Ilford, on the first day.

On the last day of the month, a Sunday, Kentishbus's 269, gained in January, was converted to midibus operation on Sundays. Optare Metrorider No. 887 from Northfleet's B11 allocation is caught in Widmore Road.

The changes to Green Line routes that affected LT were to the 726 and the new 465. The 726 was cut to Heathrow Central but retained as an LRT contract route between there and Dartford, with Kentishbus and Luton & District still the operators and with the same coaches. The only difference was the fitment of 'London Transport Service' stickers. Before the change, Kentishbus Duple-bodied Leyland Leopard 224 is seen in Bromley. London & Country's new route 465 was an LRT contract between Kingston (Ham BAC Works, Monday-Friday peaks) and Leatherhead London & Country garage, to where Leyland National SNB 383 heads a week after the changes were implemented (on 29th June). The service was extended commercially to Horsham every 2 hours: it took over from Green Line 714.

At Harrow, modifications were made to mobility routes on 31st July. Route 980 was a new Tuesday-only route introduced to serve sheltered housing in Colindeep Lane. LS 156 at Brent Cross Shopping Centre.

July

LT's Annual Business Plan was announced on 11th July and stated that there was to be a record investment programme of £603 million, an increase of £12 million over the previous year's figure. LT was expected to show an operating deficit of £110 million for the financial year 1991/92. LT's new *Statement of Strategy* was published the same day for the period 1991-1994, following several months of consultation with the relevant authorities, and about 1600 opinions from members of the public. Among the major priorities were safety, promoting efficiency through bus route tendering and promoting the role of the bus prior to deregulation by improving service quality, working for bus priority measures and advocating a fairer allocation of road space.

London Buses announced a programme of London-wide bus stop cleaning, and awarded a contract for it to London Underground's Cleaning Services department, the same department that was already in the business of cleaning bus shelters.

Two extensively refurbished Routemasters, RML 2648 from London General's Victoria garage and RML 2735 from CentreWest's Westbourne Park garage, were unveiled this month. Modifications included fitment of new headlights, indicators and stop-lights, new destination blind and interior lighting using high-intensity fluorescent lighting, refurbishment of the rear 'B' frame and replacement of outdated brake-slack adjusters, accumulators and steering side-arm bodies. The interiors and heating systems of the two buses were also given extensive refurbishment, and altogether London Buses is looking to gain an extra ten years' service out of them. Market research was to be carried out before London Buses took a decision on refurbishing the rest of the Routemaster fleet. Where to see them: RML 2735 is on the 7 (East Acton – Holborn, terminating at Red Lion Square) and 15 (Westbourne Park Garage—East Ham, but going no

On 20th July, Plumstead held their open day, where five year old museum piece Optare Star Rider OV 2 was presented by Selkent MD Bryan Constable (standing on the right) to the London Transport Museum, very attractively restored to original Roundabout colours of grey and maroon.

further eastwards than Aldgate) while the other one is (officially) confined to the 11 (Shepherds Bush – Liverpool Street Station). I think the only other thing comparable to the vast following of the Routemaster (that's everyone from the enthusiast to the ordinary person in the street) is the love and affection the public has for the equine hero of National Hunt horse racing, Desert Orchid. Both 'Dessie' and the LBL Routemaster fleet have had tremendous amounts of money splashed out on them.

More on the up-and-down fortunes of London United's Airbus operation, because from 20th July the A3, from Stamford Brook (bus garage – every journey a live garage run!) via Chiswick, Hammersmith, Kensington High Street, Marble Arch, Marylebone Road, Camden Town, Walthamstow and the M11 to Stansted Airport, providing an eight-times a day service (six on Sundays) from Central London to London's third airport, took off. It crash-landed precisely two months later. Also on the roads, new Mobility Bus services commenced in the Hillingdon and Hounslow areas from July 29th, using MT-class Mercedes 709Ds bodied by Reeve-Burgess, with wheelchair accomodation, from Uxbridge garage. Also revisions to Harrow Mobility routes required the allocation of another wheelchair-carrying midibus, the Victoria Basement' s CVE Omni CV 4, previously used on the Central London Carelink service.

London Forest again: after a one-day stoppage on 4th July, London Forest came out on indefinite strike from 11th. This situation lasted for 19 days, but brought about some most interesting operations as the photograph section will show you.

But it wasn't all bad. London General bus driver Ray Hayter won the title of London Buses' Bus Driver of The Year for the fourth time, in LBL's annual competition held at Battersea Park on 21st July.

The London Forest strike resulted in some unfamiliar workings. Ensign Citybus Metrobus No. 281 at Waterloo on the D1 on 15th July, Kentishbus Roe-bodied Atlantean 681 at Leyton on route 56 (going no further west than Clapton Pond) on the same day and their Olympian 530 also at Leyton on the same service.

The revised Harrow area routes all began on 19th January, bringing many colours to Harrow' s roads. Our picture shows the colours of Sovereign Bus & Coach's Mercedes 811s, acquired by London Country (North West)'s green and grey 9.8-metre Dennis Darts bodied by Carlyle for route 258. With the take-over of LCNW by Luton & District, the latter buses later appeared with L & D fleetnames on the front and 'Watfordwide' fleetnames on the sides, this being the trading name for their Watford services, but the 258 and 340 routes come from the same garage. The Dart was taken at Harrow Hill in May.

The Wandsworth scheme in all its glory. The DR class entered service for the first time, and a very smart DR 4 was also caught in May, on the H37, the renumbered Hounslow-Richmond part of the erstwhile 37 route.

The first Titans allocated to South London went to Norwood to release Metrobuses needed for Wandsworth routes and entered service from Norwood in May. T 269 was photographed in July at Waterloo carrying South London's name and logo and plain upper-deck front windows.

Route 123 was covered by two operators, between Gants Hill and Tottenham Hale only. London Buslines Olympian No. 38 and Grey-Green Volvo Citybus E105JYV (normally used on Kent commuter routes) are seen at the Gants Hill end. County Bus & Coach's Essex contract route 505 gained extra buses, authorised by LRT, to cover the busy Walthamstow—Chingford corridor. Normally a midibus route, County's National SN 604 provides the capacity badly needed on the service at Walthamstow Central on 15th July.

South of the Thames, at Bexleyheath a new midibus type to the garage arrived when MTLs (Mercedes-Benz 811Ds with Reeve Burgess bodywork) were allocated there. MTL 1, formerly of Uxbridge, is caught in Tom Cribb Road on 20th July 1991.

An award for initiative, at least, should go to London United for the A3 service to Stansted, which started on 15th July and finished two months later. The three coach-seated Olympians from Stamford Brook's 237 allocation were signwritten for it. L 314 at Lancaster Terrace runs through drizzle in August.

To fill the gaps on the 237, Metrobuses appeared. M 1190 with Airbus sign-writing itself and super-imposed blinds, loads at Hounslow.

Some enthusiasts didn't think a lot of these! Kent Engineering converted some of London Coaches' RCLs to convertible open-top, an effective wheeze that enabled all-year round use with a reduced amount of vehicles, but it's their appearance that seems to be bugging Routemaster enthusiasts. They were done in May and June: RCL 2240 is caught at London Bridge.

County's Darts could be seen on the 444 as well as the W16: this route directly took over from London Forest's route 144. DP 308 is caught in Silver Street, Walthamstow on 29th November.

As always, CentreWest are the greatest purveyors of innovation where bus services are concerned. From November 16th the 607 Express between Uxbridge and Shepherds Bush via the Uxbridge Road used refurbished, coachseated, DiPTAC converted, single-doored, ex-Red Arrow LSs and the ex-route 128 used Lynxes to replace Metrobuses. The striking livery applied is shown to good effect on LX 2 of Uxbridge garage, seen near Hillingdon Heath.

The world's greatest tenor, Luciano Pavarotti, a man with an even bigger voice than his body, filled Hyde Park with his free concert on 30th July despite the weather, and London Buses tried to fill their buses with homegoing fans. Five special services were organised: a service from Park Lane to Euston and Kings Cross (M 885 from Westbourne Park is on that), a service from Park Lane to Victoria and Waterloo Stations (Red Arrow LS 440 works that outside the Hilton Hotel), a route X29 express from Park Lane to Enfield (Leaside Buses M 1217 represents the one-bus allocation to it), a route X73 express to Waltham Cross that ran blindless, and a service from Park Lane to Hammersmith via route 9 which didn't actually run. Flat fares of £1 and £2 generally applied. Altogether Pavarotti was more impressive.

London Buslines took on new routes 201 and the 203 from Westlink at the same time. The existing 203 (basically Staines to Hounslow) continued via Stanwell twice an hour, with an hourly deviation via Bedfont Green and Staines Road as route 201, thus meaning a combined 20-minute service. Between Hounslow and Brentford the route was discontinued. The midibuses required for it (brand new Mercedes 811Ds with Reebur bodywork were ordered) were not forthcoming at the start of operations, so Dodge 50s were hired from South Yorkshire at first. It was around September when the Mercs arrived, and No. 631 is on the 201 here on the A30 Great South West Road, on 18th October.

August

The first London Buses subsidiary to be sold was announced on 2nd August as London Coaches, as was much speculated beforehand. London Coaches operate the sightseeing tour with Routemasters, plus some Kent commuter coach services and a contract for the Japanese School in Acton, among other private hires and excursions.

It may or may not have seemed inevitable, but London Forest lost its Walthamstow area contract routes. The T & GWU claimed the decision by the Tendered Bus Unit a victory. London Forest's MD Tom Young still believed the company had a future, and said: "I would be surprised if more than 100 (of around 300 people laid off) get jobs with winning contractors." Then, on the 20th, Mr. Young resigned from his post and was replaced by LBL Network Services Manager Graham Elliott, who was appointed as acting managing director.

Meanwhile at Selkent, the commercial director Ken Glazier (a well-known transport historian) announced that he was taking early retirement as of 6th September. Mr. Glazier spent 40 years working with London Transport and its successors (referring to the pre-1984 LT – as readers probably know, today's London Regional Transport has once again adopted the more familiar form of title for day-to-day use).

New to the fray this month was Tellings Golden Miller, a Drawlane subsidiary, and thanks to them the Leyland National made a comeback on to LRT tendered routes as the under seven-years-old rule for buses used on such routes was thrown out.

Westlink regained a toehold on the Staines Road corridor of the 116 and 117 by commercially registering this route, the 417 from Hounslow Bus Station via Ashford Hospital to Egham, running hourly on Mondays to Saturdays. Two Leyland Nationals were required: LS 408 passes the 'Hussar' at Hounslow Heath.

Metrobus of Orpington ordered seven Reebur-bodied Darts, and with the newly taken on 146 only needing two, the new buses also operated their successful commercial service 351, between Bromley North and Penge. The route needed a capacity increase: J702EMX provides it here at Penge.

Additional Sunday services on the 493, before and after the normal Sunday timetable, were also operated commercially by Metrobus, on London Bus Agreement, not as part of the LT contract. Metrobus used its new Darts on these journeys—J702EMX stops at the Spur Road—picking up passengers.

Another change of operator was route 493, from Kentishbus to London & Country on 17th August. AN-class Atlanteans were the norm, with appearances by Volvo Citybuses. AN 196 here has just departed the Walnut Centre in Orpington.

London Coaches may have been up for sale, but carried on operations regardless with the introduction of 'London Plus', an expansion of the existing sightseeing tour. In summer, this used ERM extended Routemaster open-toppers, but the brief winter London Plus operation—it was withdrawn in December—was with RMAs, such as 15 seen at Tower Hill in December.

Still on the sightseeing theme: a new operator made its debut in August with a diverse mix of buses. The Big Bus Company introduced its version of the London sightseeing tour with buses carrying a traditional-style cream and maroon livery. Illustrated here at the Tower are an ex-East Kent AEC Regent V dating from 1959 with its Park Royal body converted to open top, PFN853, and one of the many B20 DMSs sold by London Buses during the year, ex-DMS 2361.

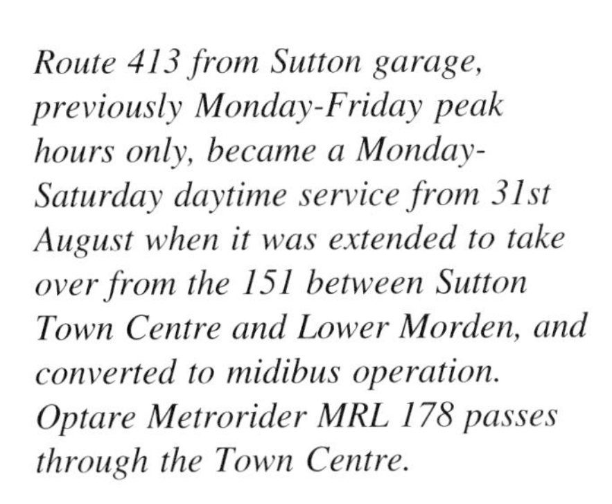

Route 413 from Sutton garage, previously Monday-Friday peak hours only, became a Monday-Saturday daytime service from 31st August when it was extended to take over from the 151 between Sutton Town Centre and Lower Morden, and converted to midibus operation. Optare Metrorider MRL 178 passes through the Town Centre.

London Central expanded their 'Lakeside Clipper' idea in August by introducing new Lakeside Clipper 701X from Bricklayers Arms via Surrey Quays, Greenwich and Woolwich to the Lakeside Shopping Centre on the outskirts of Grays, running on Wednesdays and Saturdays. Olympian L 95, being the registration number originally carried by Routemaster RM29, has just commenced its journey here.

**The 197 group of routes and the 403 were subject to alterations from August 31st. New route 407 took over from them between Wallington and West Croydon (ex 403) and West Croydon and Caterham Valley (ex 197A/B). From Croydon garage, Leyland Olympian L 255 represents the normal allocation to the route at Purley.*

*Right: *The128's replacement in the Hertfordshire area was sorted out by Hertfordshire County Council, who put out to tender new Monday-Saturday route R1 linking up Harefield, Mount Vernon Hospital, Rickmansworth and Chorleywood. None other than LBL subsidiary CentreWest won the tender, and the route was allocated to Uxbridge garage! Originally a temporary situation, it lasted into 1992. MA 80 here turns at Harefield.*

*Far right: *A replacement for the Sunday variation, 128A (Uxbridge to Harefield Hospital via Hillingdon Station and Ruislip, hourly) was four-round-trips route U8 over the same roads. MA 87 is seen near West Ruislip with a typical load, i.e. not a lot.*

From 1977 to 1991—the Hillingdon Local Service 128 ran for the last time on 16th August. Their replacements are illustrated here.

** To retain the Ruislip to Harefield Hospital service, route U1 received an hourly extension on to Harefield Hospital, increasing to half-hourly in the peak hours. Merc/Alexander MA 48 approaches the 'Coach & Horses' in Ickenham.*

** To provide some increased capacity in the wake of the 128's withdrawal, peak-hour big-bus journeys were introduced onto the U1 schedule with just one Leyland National comprising the allocation. LS 484 was redundant from the Red Arrow fleet and so was converted to single door and upseated for the job. Looking as fresh and clean as Uxbridge's buses always seem to do, it is caught here at the Swakeleys Roundabout.*

Another one of those strange workings, supposed to be a Dennis Dart, but in fact Metrobus M 36, on midi route H91 at Hounslow West on 15th August .

Docklands Light Railway engineering work severely overran during the period following the August Bank Holiday. On the resulting replacement bus service, Ensign Citybus Metrobus No. 286 is caught at the Tower on 28th August. Various London Buses buses were also to be seen. ITV's Teletext page giving LT service information reported extra buses on route D1, though this was not the case.

Ensign Citybus took on the ex London Forest routes 97A and 215 in Walthamstow from 14th September. Leyland Olympian No. 122 on the 97A carries Alexander bodywork.

September

The main event of the month was the announcement by London Buses on 16th September to disband the London Forest subsidiary, following a review of the company's viability after the loss of the Walthamstow routes. London Forest was also thought to have limited prospects for success in winning future tenders. Although it was originally thought that Leyton garage was to close, it was decided instead to close Walthamstow and ten-year-old Ash Grove garages. Numerous reallocations of London Forest routes took place, and these will be looked at in the November section.

No doubt these events were at the back of LT chairman Wilfrid Newton's mind when he laid the foundation stone of Centre West, not the LBL subsidiary, but the biggest property development in West London. Previously only known to me as a huge eyesore in the middle of Hammersmith, Centre West occupies the Broadway site in the centre of the one-way system, covering all of six acres. New undercover interchange facilities will include a new bus station linked to a modernised Underground station for the District and Piccadilly Lines, and by the existing subway to the nearby Hammersmith & City Line station. When completed it will also feature 470,000 square feet of offices in two buildings and a 65,000 square-foot shopping centre.

LT announced on 5th September that they were to link up with map-producers Cook, Hammond and Kell on a new series of 36 computerised local bus maps. This revolutionary method of map production was expected to significantly reduce costs and time spent drawing them, because previously all maps had to be hand-drawn, and apparently just one mistake could mean that the whole thing had to be re-drawn!

I must have seen more information on proposed bus-priority ideas than any other subject concerned with London's buses. A report from the London Planning Advisory Committee (LPAC) published on September 4th and entitled *Green Routes – Report on Bus Priority* said that bus lanes and other bus priority measures could provide benefits to the community valued at up to 15 times the cost of implementing them. The LPAC's report was based on observations in the London Boroughs of Hammersmith & Fulham, Hounslow, Kensington & Chelsea, Lambeth, Richmond and Wandsworth. The study concluded by saying that comprehensive bus priority schemes could be introduced to the great majority of bus routes, so that they could become true 'green' routes.

More computer services for LBL: computer services company Hoskyns Group PLC signed a multi-million pound three-year contract with London Buses to provide an Information Technology service. Eventually. responsibility for IT operation will be transferred to the London Buses subsidiaries, but for the time being the contract enables London Buses to concentrate on its core business during the run-up to deregulation.

New on the roads: in Walthamstow routes 97A and 215 became the first to be lost by London Forest, both going to Ensign Citybus, while East London commenced a new localised route scheme of its own based on Barking. Also with East London,. 23.rd September saw the commencement of three new Docklands Light Railway supplementary bus services, to provide a guaranteed service in case the railway failed. Unreliability on the DLR was the main factor behind the introduction of the service. Twenty brand new Scania N133/ Alexander 'deckers (S 10-29) were ordered for it, but none arrived by the end of September. Most did not enter service until November.

London United's Norbiton garage closed on 5th September, its remaining routes going to Fulwell. LBL's Westlink subsidiary, following the loss the previous month of routes 116, 117 and 203 and the laying off it was to hold on to 23 LSs that came off service as a result as it was going to look for new tenders.

Ensign Citybus Northern Counties-bodied Olympian No. 133 was a one-off purchase from 1989, and it is seen here on ex-London Forest route 215.

At the same time Ensign received six new Northern Counties-bodied Olympians for use in Walthamstow. This one, in the correct Capital Citybus colours for that area, but not for Romford area routes is seen at Hornchurch (White Hart) on route 252.

Twenty-three buses for two workings on its new route were needed 417.

Grey-Green took on evening and Sunday services on Thamesway's routes 167 and 275 from 22nd September, due to staff problems being experienced by the latter. However, Thamesway had solved their problems by 5th October, from which date they resumed the full service. Two Grey-Green single-deck Volvo B10M models of the specially-built 10.3-metre type with East Lancs bodywork from the route 210 allocation, Nos. 917 and 913, are caught on the routes on 29th September.

Thamesway introduced new Mercedes 709Ds to its oldest contract route, the 193 (oldest that is if you count the time from when Eastern National took it on originally to when Thamesway was formed) taking over from older Mercedes 608s (the van conversions) and here at Hornchurch (White Hart) is No. 0390.

East London introduced a new localised network in Barking from 14th September, with sections of routes withdrawn and replaced by new routes in a 'B' series. Routes are B1 (Barking, Thames View Estate to Little Heath), B2 (Barking, Thames View Estate to Mayesbrook Park, illustrated here, with Titan T184 on duty) B3 (Barking to Marks Gate) and B4 (Mon-Fri only, Becontree Heath to Creekmouth).

Over in Surrey Westlink have always seemed to be good at obtaining contract services for the County Council. In September they took on four new contracts: the 572 (Sundays, Kingston to Englefield Green), 578 (Sundays, Kingston to Leatherhead), 582 (Sundays, Kingston to Heathrow Central) and 661 (Schooldays, West Molesey to Hinchley Wood School). At Hampton Station, MCW Metroliner MRL 79 works on the 572, whilst loading up at Central Square in West Molesey is Titan T 935 on the 661, with 'lazy' destination blind.

Over to the west, Route 224 became a 'Midilink' with Alexander-bodied Mercedes from Alperton garage. They came from the Gold Arrow routes at Westbourne Park and, thanks to repaints, looked none the worse. MA105 here at Iveagh Avenue.

A strange working. From the defunct 128 allocation at Uxbridge, Leyland Lynx LX 11 turns up on the 223 at West Drayton on 11th September.

To release vehicles for the new DLR supplementary bus service, West Ham's route D3 had to be converted to LS operation, using a motley collection of vehicles from all over the shop. Single-door LS 27 is an ex-Forester bus (remember the X99? It was only in 1986!) which had also gone to London Coaches briefly: it came from London Northern for the D3, though how the 253 RM via blind came to be in its blind box, I have no idea! Caught in the Commercial Road.

Noteworthy new buses to enter service were London Central's DRLs, the 9-metre version of the very attractive Reeve Burgess 'Pointer'-bodied Dennis Dart. Here is DRL 1 'Del Boy' seen in Peckham soon after entering service.

October

Yet another advertising scheme to 'get London moving', this time by LT, was announced on 3rd October. It was aimed at drivers who park illegally or stop at bus stops, on yellow lines or in bus lanes. And the slogan? 'We'll get London moving if everyone's on board.' Advertisements appeared on local radio and on buses and bus shelters. One poster contained the phrase 'When your bus turns up late, make sure you blame the right drivers.' It featured a picture of a van unloading at a bus stop, a scenario that any London bus drivers reading this probably finds all too familiar.

The annual fare increase was announced on 15th October. Single fares on the Underground and Docklands Light Railway were to be put up 10p (longer distance journeys 20p) whilst on the buses the daytime fare structure (i.e. after the morning peak) was to be simplified so that, for example, outside central London just two fares existed on most routes – 40p and 60p. The one-day six-zone off peak Travelcard (the one that I would recommend you buy if you ever want to come to London for a day and see a few buses) was to go up to £3.40 from £3.10: a weekly six-zoner was to go to £23.80 from £22.00. The LT Card was to remain unchanged.

That forward thinking, forward moving, east London area bus operator, the ubiquitous Ensign Citybus, announced that they had abolished the use of company cars for senior staff and their MD, Leon Daniels, called on other bus operators to do the same.

East London commenced their campaign to make its buses cleaner by placing notices on its buses asking passengers to take their litter home. East London apparently spend £65,000 a year on the daily cleaning of bus interiors.

The main event on the roads came from London Central, who introduced their new DRL-class 9 metre Dennis Darts with Reeve-Burgess Pointer bodywork to its Peckham midibus routes which are LRT contracts. The first four of them were named after characters in the great BBC comedy series 'Only Fools and Horses' which is set in Peckham. First day was October 5th.

Another of the new Dart-Reeve Burgess buses, DRL7 is seen on Peckham route P12.

County Bus & Coach took on the W16, also with Reebur-bodied Dennis Darts. DP 301 is caught in Lea Valley Road, with blind badly set.

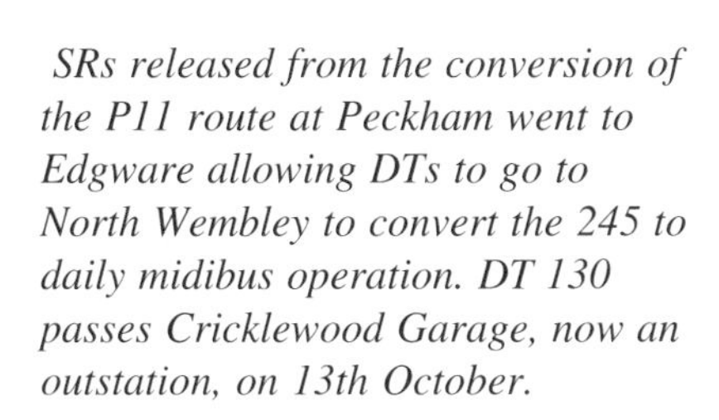

SRs released from the conversion of the P11 route at Peckham went to Edgware allowing DTs to go to North Wembley to convert the 245 to daily midibus operation. DT 130 passes Cricklewood Garage, now an outstation, on 13th October.

Between October 2nd and November 3rd, the duration of the Rugby World Cup, for matches at Twickenham London United provided special services and some Metrobuses at Fulwell garage received special advertising to that effect. When not required for such services, of course they could be seen on normal stage use like M 828 here on the 267 on 18th October. Also most noteworthy are the (almost) old-style upper case via points.

Capital Citybus took over the remainder of its ex-London Forest routes in Walthamstow, the 97, 158 and 212. Here, and overleaf, are some of the vehicles used: Dennis Dominator No. 269, was repainted from Ensign blue and silver colours.

November

The major event of the month was the announcement by London Buses of new vehicle orders for fleet replacement, which called for 19 Optare Deltas to go to East London, 16 Dennis Lances, and on the double-deck front 22 Optare Spectras and 40 Northern Counties-bodied Scanias, though the latter total increased to 42 if you include two for London Northern at Potters Bar which had in fact been ordered previously. East London's Deltas were to go to Seven Kings, along with the demonstrator, taken into stock as DA 10, to replace Titans on routes 129 and 148, and of the Scanias Ss 30 and 31 arrived before the year end and were the ones allocated to Potters Bar. They entered service in December. Meanwhile London Buses continued to experiment with demonstrators, the latest of which turned up at Uxbridge for the duration 5th-9th November before moving on to Holloway, then Waterloo (Red Arrow) and Streatham, in the shape of MAN/Optare Vecta H846 UUA.

Armchair, operators of routes 65 and 260, were in court over 200 charges of excessive hours worked by drivers. However, proceedings by the Metropolitan Police against Armchair were adjourned until December 2nd to allow Armchair's solicitors more time to prepare the defence.

The introduction of 'Passenger Information at Bus Stops' (PIBS) to route 18 between Kings Cross and Sudbury took a step closer this month when London Transport signed a £700,000 contract with French company Serel, of Nice, to provide the hardware, software and signs required. The signs are to be of a type similar to existing dotmatrix train indicators on the Underground and are to go on 50 of the busier stops on the route, giving detailed information about route 18 plus basic info on other routes serving the stop with digital speech units to help visually-handicapped passengers, who can request the unit to 'speak' the information. Under a separate

contract with Serel, the automatic vehicle location equipment and associated technological gizmos, such as microwave beacons and transponders, are also to be supplied. When it's all running, the equipment will be able to locate buses with an accuracy of 10 to 20 metres, and it's expected to begin in the Summer of '92.

This month saw the commencement by London Transport Bus Passenger Infrastructure, the managers of London's bus stations and stops, of a programme to appoint 'Controllers' to major bus

More Capital Citybus vehicles on former London Forest routes:- Northern Counties-bodied Olympian No. 132, having been 'run-in' on Havering services. Ensign/Capital's sole ex-Derby Metrobus, numbered 112, still in Ensign colours.

County Bus and Coach took route W15, from London Forest. This route left the majority of Walthamstow's MRLs looking quite rough after their three years: it is a very busy route and I just wonder how these slightly less well-built Mercedes 811s will cope. MD 602 carries a good load here.

stations. Controllers are to provide a more 'human' face and an on-site presence passengers and help in the management of the bus station – this latter discipline includes updating of publicity and timetable displays. The controllers also liaise with the local bus companies operating in that area to keep abreast of service changes and assist with passengers' problems. The first appointments were at Golders Green and Walthamstow bus stations, both daily, with more to follow.

London Transport announced that the smoking ban on London's buses had been a success. Surveys showed that 71% of passengers were in favour of the ban and 12% disliked it, with 85% of non-smokers in favour. Conclusive proof that the smoker is in the minority these days. Following the success of that, London Buses commenced a poster campaign to make buses even healthier still. Posters appeared on buses and shelters dissuading bus passengers from eating their cod and chips (or

Thamesway, although regaining route W13, lost the W14 to County Bus & Coach: however they gained routes W11 and W12 from London Forest and were in a position to re-deploy their Mercedes 709Ds, which would otherwise have been made redundant.
** Thamesway 0255 approaches the turn out of South Countess Road in fading light.*
** 0258 passes Eagle Pond in Snaresbrook Road in wispy sunlight.*
** County introduced their own Merc 709s to the W14, though interspersed with ex-Welwyn Hatfield Line Optare City Pacers at first. This one is numbered MB 933 and it is caught at Wanstead.*

cheese-burger or veggie-burger or whatever, take your pick) on the buses and then leaving the packaging on the bus. LBL haven't banned eating altogether, but they tried to appeal to the minority who don't realise that they may be annoying other passengers by so doing, so passengers were encouraged to eat up before getting on the bus and binning their litter or taking it home.

And now the award for 'Nice Try of The Year' goes to Yorkshire Rider, who get a

mention in this book by virtue of announcing a bold bid to obtain the tenders on routes 119, 166, 194, 198 and 227 in the Bromley and Croydon areas, using 65 brand new buses. Sadly (for YR), the bid fell flat as the routes were awarded to Selkent, with the exception of the 227 which went to Kentishbus.

November 23rd was the day that London Forest ended, and its remnants were reorganised. Routes, buses and garages that remained open were distributed amongst Leaside Buses, who

The gap in T 297's white band is where the London Forest tree logo had been: the tree has been uprooted and replaced by the mute swan logo of Leaside Buses, underneath the windscreen. Leaside took on a quantity of 'Forest Titans and allocated them to Stamford Hill. . .

. . . .which released some Metrobuses for the new regime on the 106 in lieu of Ash Grove Titans. Allocated to Clapton garage, M 660 leads a pair in Amhurst Road, Hackney on 5th **December.**

gained Clapton garage and routes 38 (Mon-Sat), 106, 236, Ash Grove's share of route 253 and Essex County Council routes 211 and 213 from Waltham Cross to Breach Barns and Upshire respectively; East London, who gained Leyton garage and routes 30, 48, 230, 257, D1, D6, 38 (Sun

Established Clapton inmates since May 27th 1989 were the RMLs on the 38 and the MRLs on the 236 (and W15 until November): Leaside Buses took on the lot. MRL 119 is seen on a foggy old morning at Finsbury Park.

A right old swap-around concerned the RML allocations on routes 6 and 8. Metroline's Willesden garage gained the lion's share of the 6, with the minority allocation going to East London at Bow. This meant that Bow had to lose some of their complete allocation on the 8 —which went to Metroline! Representing their expansion in crew operation, Metroline's RML 2594 from Willesden is seen on the 8 in Bishopsgate.

OPO allocation), the Leyton Mobility Bus network plus part of route 6, the lion's share allocation of which went to Metroline along with a share of East London's own route 8; and London Central, who assumed all of route 35. Ash Grove and Walthamstow garages were closed. A considerable number of other changes made November the busiest month of the year, as my illustrations depict.

The Sunday OPO operation on the 6 moved from Ash Grove to Willesden, and Metrobus M 184 is seen on that in Regent Street.

Yet another Metroline gain was night route N6, also previously from Ash Grove. This meant that one of the major beneficiaries from the London Forest disbanding operated its buses to the very centre of the turmoil, Walthamstow, albeit at night. The first Metroline bus to serve Walthamstow was M 1431 early on the morning of the 23rd.

Another subsidiary to gain Titans was South London, enabling them to pension off DMSs ahead of their time. (That's just what I think—I've got a fair idea what the rest of you think about DMSs!) Allocated to Brixton and Croydon garages, the former's T 357 is seen near Streatham Hill, while the latter's T 534 is seen in Addiscombe Road. The route on which T 534 is operating was one of three lost to Selkent on tender, which is expected to result in ructions during 1992.

While Capital Citybus gained in Walthamstow, they lost one of their more firmly-established routes. The 62 was taken back by London Buses through their East London subsidiary from 23rd November. It's remarkable that the last RTs came off this route in April 1979, it was taken over by RMs and then, a matter of months later, taken over by crew Titans. From that same batch of Titans, OPO (naturally) T 204 from Barking garage, loads up in Woodward Road.

Expansion of bus services to Docklands was a feature of new developments. London Central's route 40 was rerouted away from its normal Monday-Friday terminus at Poplar (Blackwall Tunnel) to serve Canary Wharf from 25th November. T 1001 pauses at lights at London Bridge.

The Beckton Express X15 lost its RMCs in favour of OPO Titans from 23rd November, but at least there were more journeys on this popular commuter service. T 286 loads up at East Beckton (Asda) on 3rd December. The buses, decked out in standard red with gold relief, interworked onto new Monday-Friday daytime route D10 from Liverpool Street to Canary Wharf, a new route to Docklands. T 653 pauses for a moment to pick up at Liverpool Street on 5th December: it left empty.

From November 30th part one of the LT Wood Green scheme introduction of route W4 between Wood Green and Tottenham Hale on Mondays to Saturdays. A Sunday service is expected to follow in 1992 with the introduction of the rest of the scheme. Brand new MRL 210 looks anything but new in dense fog!

East London converted routes 241 and 278 to midibus on the same date, with one return big-bus journey on schooldays as 378. Because MRL 70 (West Ham) has no rear blind box, the intending passengers have to go up to the front to see if it's their bus: coach seated MRL 132 reveals its oil filler cap, and T 614 on the school journey 378 causes an impatient driver to go round it,rather than wait.

London Northern's route 46 was converted from Titan operation to Mercedes-Benz 811D Optare Starrider SR midibuses from 16th November. Branded Midilink, Chalk Farm's SR 9, formerly of Peckham (hence the unremoved London Central fleetname) loads up at Kings Cross.

Here's a change that was proposed over a year ago. From 16th November the H40 was finally introduced to take over from the E4, running between Park Royal Asda and Turnham Green. From Stamford Brook garage, ex-Walthamstow MCW Metrorider MRL 120 arrives at Park Royal.

Route 27 commenced its LRT contract from 9th November with London United, but was shortened to run Camden Town to Turnham Green only. As a result the 391 gained an extension to Richmond to replace the truncated portion of the 27, a frequency increase on the 135 sufficing at the other end. It also meant the introduction of the 391 on Sundays, the operation of which was won on tender by R & I Tours (London United operates it Monday-Saturday) using their Carlyle-bodied Dennis Darts from the C11/C12 allocation. R & I No. 229 pauses at Turnham Green, having just worked from Richmond.

Route 108B and part of route 75 were replaced by new midibus route 202 from 23rd November, running between Crystal Palace and Blackheath (Royal Standard). Associated with this, the 75 was converted to midibus operation on Sundays. Replaced on the Gold Arrow routes by DWs, an allocation of MAs went to Plumstead to operate the route: MA 20 is seen at Lee Green on 19th December.

Quite a lot happened to route 152 from 30th November. Converted to MRL midibus operation, it was truncated to terminate at New Malden at the western end, leaving the section between there and Kingston to the 131. However at the other end it was extended to the Pollards Hill Estate, replacing route 352. Operation was from Merton garage: MRL 187 is seen at New Malden. The common practice of keeping a big bus on for school journeys occurred again: Sutton provided the bus, known as 452, working between Hook and Mitcham (Cricketers). M 1215 loads up here on that journey.

Roadworks on the North Circular Road on 10th November brought widespread diversions, including one on route 226 via a low-bridge. This meant a one-off operation by DTs in lieu of Ms. DT 90 of Willesden garage loads up at Wembley Central.

Yet more changes in Docklands provided the main interest in December with the introduction of several new stage routes to shadow the DLR in lieu of the previous supplementary bus service, although route D11 was really an extension of the concept introduced with route D1 in 1990—a bus link from the City to Docklands, but terminating at Canary Wharf, which the D1 doesn't serve. Scania N113/Alexander S 24 in its Docklands Express livery is seen on London Bridge having just worked in from Canary Wharf.

December

London Transport published its first public statement outlining its future fares policy this month. Among the main points, LT believed that there was a strong case for somewhat higher fares than those in operation at the time – compared with Londoners' earnings, fares are now at historically low levels. The possible move to bus deregulation also suggests increases to more commercial fare levels. I wonder what commuters with monthly or annual Travelcards think of that? The document also proposed the further development of a fraud-resistant ticketing system, based on current practice but enhanced by modern technology – with electronic pay-as-you-ride cards, similar to Phonecards, being a possibility. LT would also wish to see road-pricing introduced.

Further to Armchair's problems (see last month) two former drivers with the company claimed in court that they were forced to work double-time or be sacked, and were given absolute discharges by Brentford magistrates. The two pleaded guilty to exceeding their daily hours and not taking a proper rest between shifts but the prosecution said that it was thanks to these two drivers that the matter had come to light. It was apparently alledged in court that all 41 drivers at Armchair had appeared to work too many hours. Company policy was to give three written warnings for minor infringements, then if a driver complained about the extra hours, he/she was sacked.

This month saw controllers appointed to two more bus stations – Finsbury Park on Mondays to Saturdays, and Turnpike Lane daily.

In Docklands, the new Scanias were redeployed on new stage routes, initiated to distinguish the different routes the Docklands Light Railway supplementary bus

Scania S 22 illustrates the conversion of the original 'Docklands Express' route from Titan operation as it leaves for Harbour Exchange Square.

Stripped of its Docklands Express signwriting and logos, Titan T 586 reverts to slightly more mundane duties on 15th December.

service took, but at the same time retaining the same routes in case of DLR failure. One of the new services introduced, the D11 between London Bridge and Canary Wharf and marketed as 'Docklands Express' was launched by Mr Patrick McLoughlin MP, Parliamentary Under-Secretary of State at the Department of Transport, at London Bridge on 9th December.

With it being December, the festive season beckoned. Now, as I write this, it seems that it came and went so quickly! Boxing Day brought about the now usual one-day operations, except there weren't so many of them this year. None the less, among them were the third operation of the once-a-year 86B by Capital Citybus in the Barking, Ilford and Dagenham areas (please note, by this time all of Ensign Citybus became officially known as Capital Citybus) and a one-day extension of the 102 northwards from Lower Edmonton to Ponders End (Enfield Bus Garage): other, more significant one-offs are illustrated. Also, New Year's Eve

The other new routes were the D8, Stratford—Crossharbour, and D9, Bank—Crossharbour (Mon-Fri evenings and all day weekends). A mixed allocation of Titans and Scanias operates these routes in practice: Scania S 11 is seen in 'normal' livery in Marsh Wall.

Working the new D9 was Titan T643—as with the Scania on D8, the lack of passengers is noteworthy.

would not be quite complete without the usual Foster's Lager-sponsored free night bus, Underground and Docklands Light Railway travel between 11.45pm and 5am on New Year's Day. And with that, so ended one of the most turbulent years in the history of London's buses.

This very smart demonstrator caught us all by surprise. MAN/Optare Vecta H846 UUA finished its stint with London Buses by taking a turn with Catford on the P4 from 18th to 20th December, management driven while there. Its use in service was surprising, though, in the light of its not being fitted with an assault screen. In a silver and blue livery, H846 UUA stands at Brixton on 19th December.

Tellings-Golden Miller found it necessary to hire buses used on the defunct Panther Corporation operation in Crawley, a troubled operation itself that found its way into the Drawlane (TGM's owners) empire. Leyland National UFG 54S, formerly of Southdown, is caught in London Road approaching Isleworth on 9th December.

And so to Boxing Day, which by comparison with 1989/90 was much less eventful. Bringing Capital Citybus to the centre of the capital, all-Leyland Olympian 148 is caught at Piccadilly Circus on Kentishbus's route 22B.

With the 1 not working to Bromley Common (Bromley garage), Roundabout route R11 was extended westward from Bromley Common (The Crown) to Bromley North for the day. Carlyle-bodied Dennis Dart DT 37 arrives.

One-day route 272B replaced routes 96, 272 and 469 in running from Woolwich to Bexleyheath via Thamesmead and Erith. With Bexleyheath garage closed, Peckham operated it with Dart-Reeve Burgess DRLs. Here are a pair of them, DRLs 16 and 8, the latter loading up whilst on the stand. Note the full blinds.

January to March 1992

To bring this account of the turbulent London Bus scene up to date, we summarise some of the main talking points in the first three months of 1992. Pundits didn't have long to wait for the year's first – on 20th January, London Buses announced that Guide Friday Ltd, the Stratford-on-Avon based operator specialising in sightseeing using open-top buses which has expanded greatly in various areas outside London over the last few years, was the preferred bidder for London Coaches.

At that stage, the bid, of around £700,000, was subject to contract and a firm of accountants was put in to check the value. On the basis of this, a drastically reduced bid of about a third of that figure was made. London Buses did not respond and, early in March, Guide Friday withdrew its offer completely. It might have been thought that such a firm would bend over backwards to get into the London tourist market, but the Managing Director commented that London Coaches "proved not to be the same company offered for sale in October by London Buses." Guide Friday decided instead to concentrate on existing open-top operators, notably in Spain, expected to be an important market this year.

As a result, the future of London Coaches seems likely to be in a management buy-out – London Buses issued a statement regretting Guide Friday's withdrawal but saying that discussions continue with the management buy-out team. (Presumably eventually **someone** will buy London Coaches, especially now at a lower price than Guide Friday thought. Far be it from me to give a certain Scottish bus-businessman ideas....) The whole episode is typical of the present-day scenario in London. One minute, something will seem a near-certainty; the next, not so.

Two major events on the roads very quickly reminded us of the key issues during 1991 – the Wood Green area tendering scheme, and the closure of Streatham garage. In Wood Green, where the area scheme took effect on 1st February, the splitting of the 29, one of London's oldest-established routes, and the 141 into two portions in each case were major elements. Perhaps the most eye-catching feature was the appearance (in both senses) of Grey-Green's remarkable rebodied Volvo B10M buses, reduced in length to accept the new East Lancs-built double-deck bodywork by simply chopping off the rear of the chassis. It will be interesting to see how drivers cope with manoeuvring so oddly-proportioned a vehicle in London traffic.

No area scheme in London would be complete nowadays without midibuses, and these included Capital Citybus's first, Mercedes-Benz 811Ds with Reebur bodywork. London Buses subsidiaries lost some work in the redistribution of routes but at least no garages closed this time.

South of the river, South London were less fortunate and, having lost contracts for four routes (166, 194, 194A and 194B) before the end of '91, closed Streatham garage at the end of operations on, aptly, Friday 13th March. Streatham was another example of a modern, well-equipped garage being closed. Although originally dating from 1913, it was extensively refurbished in the early 'eighties, re-opening in February 1987 after the investment of much money and effort.

There seems to be no end to such sad events, for Streatham is the latest of many closures, all too often of garages which had been modernised to make them more efficient. Many LBL employees must be worried about their jobs, thinking to themselves "which will be the next garage to go?"

Perhaps to inject a little light into the gloom of that day, RML895 the first 'production' Routemaster to be refurbished under the £10 million programme now in hand, worked a few turns on Streatham garage routes. A total of 486 Routemasters – virtually the entire stock of RMLs – will be dealt with during the next two years. The programme follows the exercise carried out on RML2648 and 2735 last year and follows on from the re-organising scheme under which most of the buses in question have been fitted with new Cummins or Ivaco engines in place of the original AEC units.

The most obvious changes are to the interiors, which at last receive fluorescent lights, one of the very few aspects in which the Routemaster's original specification was a little behind the times when they were built. The original Douglas Scott-designed internal colour scheme gives way to a new blue, grey and red moquette for the seats and is also used for the sides below waist level in the lower deck. Seat backs are in light grey and the ceilings and window surrounds are in a semi-matt off-white.

Structurally, the rear sub-frames are completely rebuilt but the aluminium body frames are still good and do not require attention. The front dome panels are renewed in a resilient plastic material to minimise those ugly dents from overhanging trees. A new Bendix air system is fitted and the vehicles are completely rewired, with various electric items updated. Overall, the aim is to obtain 'at least another ten years' service' to quote London Transport official newspaper *LT News.*

The sub-frame work is being done on all 486 by TB Precision Engineering in Birmingham which is also carrying out 220 of the complete refurbishments. Another 220 are going to South Yorkshire Transport at its Rotherham garage, while Leaside Buses is to deal with the remainder, drawn from its own stock.

However, we also have new buses coming along this year – not in tremendous quantity, but certainly in variety. We'll see 20 of the new Optare Spectra double-deckers with London Central, 40 Scania N113DRB double-deckers with Northern Counties bodywork are 19 Optare Delta single-deckers with East London, plus 40 Alexander-bodied Leyland Olympians for Leaside Buses. Dennis is supplying 54 more Darts (40 Reeve-Burgess Pointer and 14 Wrights) and 16 of the new Lance full-sized single-deckers, with Alexander bodywork. This adds up to 189 vehicles, which sounds quite a lot until one remembers that about twice as many new double-deckers were entering service **every** year in the early 'eighties. Still, we've already got the Ikarus-bodied DAF SB220s with London Coaches on the 726.

Late in February, it was announced that a decision on the setting-up of a new London Bus Executive to take over from London Transport the responsibility for organising bus services in London was 'imminent'. The Government had indicated its intentions along these lines last July, but LT has campaigned fiercely to retain its bus role, claiming that the creation of a separate authority would cost more. However, the announcement of the General Election meant that this, like the whole future for bus operation in London, was likely to remain unsettled until the new Government is appointed. So, as with so many things, we'll have to wait and see....

FLEET DETAILS

The following statistics are compiled from LBL fleet records: these are details of buses available for service within the LBL subsidiary companies at the end of 1991. They are listed company-by-company, garage-by-garage showing what types are allocated to each garage and how many are allocated for normal service, not the actual physical requirement (i.e. the scheduled Monday-Friday run-out). Driver-trainers, private hire vehicles and the London Coaches fleet are not shown.

Grateful thanks are due to London Buses for the information detailed below.

LONDON CENTRAL

Bexleyheath (code BX): 15 MR, 13 MRL, 4 MTL, 3 SR, 51 T 86
New Cross (NX): 15 L, 8 SR, 88 T 111
Peckham (PM): 16 DRL, 3 LS, 44 RM, 32 RML, 13 SR, 43 T 151
Camberwell (Q): 44 RM, 21 RML, 6 SR, 67 T 138
TOTAL AVAILABLE FOR SERVICE: 483

SELKENT

Orpington (OB): 13 DT, 5 MC, 12 RH 30
Plumstead (PD): 87 L, 11 MA, 15 MRL, 33 T 146
Bromley (TB): 12 LS , 7 MA , 20 MRL , 53 T 92
Catford (TL): 8 DW, 3 MA, 16 MW, 23 RM, 27 SR, 74 T 151
TOTAL AVAILABLE FOR SERVICE: 419

SOUTH LONDON

Streatham (AK): 12 DR, 63 M, 16 MR 91
Brixton (BN): 14 RM, 28 RML, 29 T 71
Norwood (N) : 34 L, 2 RM, 15 RML, 19 70
Croydon (TC): 1 D, 10 DMS, 61 L, 47 1 119
Thornton Heath (TH): 11 D, 15 DMS, 13 DT, 66 L 105
TOTAL AVAILABLE FOR SERVICE: 456

LONDON GENERAL

Sutton (A): 19 D, 30 DMS, 4 DW, 45 M, 1 MR, 8 MRL 107
Putney (AF): 34 M , 21 MA , 1 RM , 37 RML 93
Merton (AL): 1 DMS, 12 DR, 110 M, 7 MRL 130
Victoria Basement (GB): 6 MA, 3 MR, 19 MRL,
1 MTL, 9 OV, 25 SR 63
Victoria (GM): 24 M, 50 RM, 11 RML 85
Waterloo (RA, Red Arrow base): 54 LS 54
Stockwell (SW): 9 DR, 70 M, 5 RM, 10 RML, 39 VC 133
TOTAL AVAILABLE FOR SERVICE: 665

LONDON UNITED

Hounslow (AV): 24 DR, 22 DT, 8 FR, 3 LS, 59 M 166
Fulwell (FW): 39 DT, 80 M 199
Shepherds Bush (5): 42 M , 6 RM , 55 RML 103
Stamford Brook (V): 22 DT , 23 L , 2 LS , 6 LX ,
43 M, 4 MRL 100
TOTAL AVAILABLE FOR SERVICE: 438

WESTLINK

Kingston (K): 14 DWL, 16 MR, 15 MRL, 15 T 60
Stanwell Buses (SB, based in Green Lane,
Hounslow): 3 CV, 8 DA, 1 FS, 27 S 36
TOTAL AVAILABLE FOR SERVICE: 96

CENTREWEST

Acton Tram Depot (AT): 23 RW 23
Hanwell (HL): 51 M, 8 MA, 5 MT, 67 RW 131
Alperton (ON): 14 DW, 32 M, 10 MA 56
Uxbridge (UX): 10 LS, 5 LX, 33 M, 41 MA, 2 MT 91
Westbourne Park (X): 70 DW, 34 M, 24 MA,
6 RM, 29 RML 163
TOTAL AVAILABLE FOR SERVICE: 464

METROLINE

Willesden (AC): 8 DT, 57 M, 2 RM, 40 RML 107
Edgware (EW): 7 DT, 60 M, 19 SR 86
Harrow Weald (HD): 1 CV, 44 DT , 3 LS , 44 M 92
Cricklewood (W): 39 M 39
TOTAL AVAILABLE FOR SERVICE: 324

LONDON NORTHERN

Chalk Farm (CF): 2 MA, 10 SR, 55 T 67
Finchley (FY): 31 M, 24 RML, 24 T 79
Holloway (HT): 86 M, 5 MRL, 6 RM, 15 RML 112
Potters Bar (PB): 55 M, 9 MR, 11 5, 11 SR, 3 V 89
TOTAL AVAILABLE FOR SERVICE: 347

LEASIDE BUSES

Palmers Green (AD): 49 M 49
Tottenham (AR): 52 M, 2 RM, 47 RML 101
Clapton (CT): 2 LS, 14 M, 2 MR, 13 MRL, 4 RM, 42 RML 77
Enfield (E): 2 LS, 104 M 106
Stamford Hill (SF): 39 M, 35 T 74
Wood Green (WN): 15 DW , 95 M , 3 MR 113
TOTAL AVAILABLE FOR SERVICE: 520

EAST LONDON

Seven Kings (AP): 1 DA, 1 RN, 65 T 67
Barking (BK): 93 T 93
Bow (BW): 33 RB, 4 RM, 41 RML, 46 T 124
North Street (Romford) (NS): 1 D, 4 LS, 1 LSL, 56 T 62
Leyton (T): 2 LS, 78 T 80
Upton Park (U): 8 RM, 49 RML, 53 T 110
West Ham (WH): 13 LS, 2 MR, 16 MRL, 20 5, 98 T 149
TOTAL AVAILABLE FOR SERVICE: 685

Remarks: LS allocations at Peckham, Harrow Weald and North Street, LSL at North Street, MT at Uxbridge and CV at Harrow Weald are for mobility bus routes.
Harrow Weald's DT allocation is outstationed at a location in North Wembley, but officially allocated at Harrow Weald.
Cricklewood is regarded as an outstation of Edgware and buses alternate between garages for maintenance reasons. The D on North Street's allocation is in fact attached to East London's private hire department, also based there. However that department was given responsibility for school route 345 when that route was taken over in November, so the D (2600) can work the route, and has done so.